Spectacular Science Projects

JANICE VANCLEAVE'S

Insects and Spiders

MIND-BOGGLING EXPERIMENTS YOU CAN TURN INTO SCIENCE FAIR PROJECTS

SCHOLASTIC INC.
New York Toronto London Auckland Sydney
Mexico City New Delhi Hong Kong

ISBN 0-439-07781-8

Published by Scholastic Inc., 555 Broadway, New York, NY 10012,
by arrangement with John Wiley and Sons, Inc.
SCHOLASTIC and associated logos are trademarks
and/or registered trademarks of Scholastic Inc.

12 11 10 9 8 7 6 5 4 3   9/9 0 1 2 3 4/0

Printed in the U.S.A.   23

First Scholastic printing, March 1999

Design by Navta Associates, Inc.
Illustrations by Doris Ettlinger

CONTENTS

DEDICATION

It is with much pleasure that I dedicate this book to Becky Rockey of the Texas Science Hotline, sponsored by the University of Texas Health Science Center at San Antonio. Becky has not only been helpful in finding facts about insects and spiders for this book, but has provided much encouragement to me. Thanks, Becky!

ACKNOWLEDGMENTS

I wish to express my appreciation to the following parents and children of a Waco, Texas, home school co-op for assisting me in testing the experiments in this book. They are: Sheila, David, Aaron, AnnaLauren, and Skylar Hunt; and Ron, Anne, Sarah, Benjamin, and Rebecca Skrabanek.

A special note of appreciation to my husband, Wade, for being so patient about having insects and spiders in various containers throughout our home. He even overlooked the mealworms that were kept in our refrigerator. Sorry, Wade! There is no immediate reprieve in sight. My next book will also have some creepy and crawly sections, as it will be about scientists and their different experiments.

ATTENTION

Obtaining Insects and Spiders

You may need to purchase insects or spiders that don't occur naturally in your area or are not available during the season you choose to do the project. See the Appendix of this book for a list of catalog suppliers of insects and spiders. Check with suppliers before deciding on a specific insect or spider, as it may not be available during some seasons.

Handling Insects and Spiders

Handle all insects and spiders in the experiments with care so that you do not harm them. Return insects and spiders you collected outdoors to the general area where you found them. Do not release purchased insects outdoors unless they are a normal part of that environment. In particular, be sure *not* to release purchased insects outdoors that are a pest to the environment, such as mealworms.

Make plans for the fate of insects that cannot be released before you purchase them. Some insects, such as butterflies, can live out their lives indoors. Others, such as mealworms, can be used as food for other organisms like fish and lizards. But insects that are pests, such as mealworms, or those not **indigenous** (native to your area) to where you live, can be humanely killed by placing the container holding them in a freezer overnight.

CAUTION: Some insects or spiders may bite or sting. Do not touch any insect or spider unless you are sure it is harmless. Check the field guides in the Appendix for information about the safe handling of insects and spiders. If in doubt, do not touch.

Introduction

Science is a search for answers. Science projects are good ways to learn more about science as you search for the answers to specific problems. This book will give you guidance and provide ideas, but you must do your part in the search by planning experiments, finding and recording information related to the problem, and organizing the data collected to find the answer to the problem. Sharing your findings by presenting your project at science fairs will be a rewarding experience if you have properly prepared for the exhibit. Trying to assemble a project overnight results in frustration, and you cheat yourself out of the fun of being a science detective. Solving a scientific mystery, like solving a detective mystery, requires planning and careful collecting of facts. The following sections provide suggestions for how to get started on this scientific quest. Start the project with curiosity and a desire to learn something new.

SELECT A TOPIC

The 20 chapters in this book focus on specific topics and suggest many possible problems to solve. Each topic has one "cookbook" experiment—follow the recipe and the result is guaranteed. Approximate metric equivalents have been given after all English measurements. Try several or all of these easy experiments before choosing the topic you like best and want to know more about. Regardless of the problem you choose to solve, what you discover will make you more knowledgeable about insects.

KEEP A JOURNAL

Purchase a bound notebook in which you will write everything relating to the project. This is your journal. It will contain your original ideas as well as ideas you get from books or from people like teachers and scientists. It will include descriptions of your experiments as well as diagrams, photographs, and written observations of all your results. Every entry should be as neat as possible and dated. Information from this journal can be used to write a report of your project, and you will want to display the journal with your completed project. A neat, orderly journal provides a complete and accurate record of your project from start to finish. It is also proof of the time you spent sleuthing out the answers to the scientific mystery you undertook to solve.

LET'S EXPLORE

This section of each chapter follows the sample experiment and provides additional questions about the problem presented in the experiment. By making small changes to some part of the sample experiment, new results are achieved. Think about why these new results might have happened.

SHOW TIME!

This section goes a step further than "Let's Explore" by offering more ideas for problems to solve and questions to answer related to the general topic of the chapter. You can use the format of the sample experiment to design your own experiment to solve the questions asked in "Let's Explore" and "Show Time!" Your own experiment should follow the sample experiment's format and include a single question about one idea, a list of necessary materials, a detailed step-by-step procedure, written results with diagrams, graphs, and charts if they seem helpful, and a conclusion answering and explaining the question. Include any information you found through research to clarify your answer. When you design your own experiments, make sure to get adult approval if supplies or procedures other than those given in this book are used.

If you want to make a science fair project, study the information listed here and after each sample experiment in the book to develop your ideas into a real science fair exhibit. Use the suggestions that best apply to the project topic you have chosen. Keep in mind that while your display represents all the work you have done, it must tell the story of the project in such a way that it attracts and holds the interest of the viewer. So keep it simple. Do not try to cram all of your information into one place.

To have more space on the display and still exhibit all your work, keep some of the charts, graphs, pictures, and other materials in your journal instead of on the display board itself.

The actual size and shape of displays can be different, depending on the local science fair officials, so you will have to check the rules for your science fair. Most exhibits are allowed to be 48 inches (122 cm) wide, 30 inches (76 cm) deep, and 108 inches (274 cm) high. These are maximum measurements and your display may be smaller than this. A three-sided backboard (see drawing) is usually the best way to display your work. Wooden panels can be hinged together, but you can also use sturdy cardboard pieces taped together to form a very inexpensive but presentable exhibit.

A good title of six to ten words with a maximum of 50 characters should be placed at the top of the center panel. The

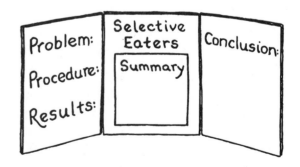

title should capture the theme of the project but should not be the same as the problem statement. For example, if the problem under question is *What type of foods do insect larvae eat?*, a good title of the project may be "Selective Eaters." The title and other headings should be neat and large enough to be readable at a distance of about 3 feet (1 m). You can glue letters to the backboard (you can use pre-cut letters that you buy or letters that you cut out of construction paper), or you can stencil the letters for all the titles. Add a short summary paragraph of about 100 words directly under the title to explain the scientific principles involved. A person who has no knowledge of the topic should be able to easily understand the basic idea of the project just from reading the summary. Have friends read the summary and ask them for their reactions. Did they understand the project? It is up to you to clarify any items that need explaining.

There are no set rules about the position of the information on the display. However, it all needs to be well organized, with the title and summary paragraph as the main point at the top of the center and the remaining material placed neatly from left to right under specific headings. Choices of headings will depend on how you wish to display the information. Separate headings for Problem, Procedure, Results, and Conclusion may be used.

The judges give points for how clearly you are able to discuss the project and explain its purpose, procedure, results, and conclusion. The display should be organized so that it explains everything, but your ability to discuss your project and answer the questions of the judges convinces them that you did the work and understand what you have done. Practice a speech in front of friends, and invite them to ask you questions. If you do not know the answer to a question, never guess or make up an answer or just say, "I don't know." Instead, you can say that you did not discover that answer during your research and then offer other information that you found of interest about the project. Be proud of the project and approach the judges with enthusiasm about your work.

CHECK IT OUT!

Read about your topic in many books and magazines. You are more likely to have a successful project if you are well informed about the topic. For the topics in this book, some tips are provided about specific places to look for information. Record in your journal all the information you find, and include for each source the author's name, the book title (or magazine name and article title), the page numbers, the publisher's name, where it was published, and the year of publication.

1

Catchers

PROBLEM

How can you catch and identify flying insects?

Materials

thin wire clothes hanger
masking tape
scissors
13-gallon (49.2-liter) tall kitchen
    plastic trash bag with straight edges
pencil
1- gallon (4-liter) resealable plastic
    vegetable bag (If a vegetable bag
    with holes is not available, use the
    point of a pencil to make 20 or 30
    small holes in a resealable plastic
    bag.)
insect field guide (See the appendix
    for a list of guides.)
helper

Procedure

1. Shape the clothes hanger into a hoop and bend the hook closed.

2. Tape the hook to form a solid handle.

3. Cut diagonally across the trash bag as shown. Keep the open-end half and discard the rest (recycle if possible).

4. Fold up about 1 inch (2.5 cm) of the cut edge of the bag and tape the fold to form a plastic net.

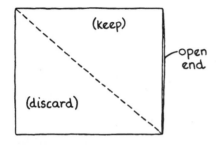

(keep)

open end

(discard)

5. Use the pencil to make 15 to 20 small holes near the bottom (pointed end) of the net. Do this by pushing the pencil through both layers of plastic.

6. Fold the edges of the open end of the plastic net over the hoop of the clothes hanger. Tape the edges inside the net as shown.

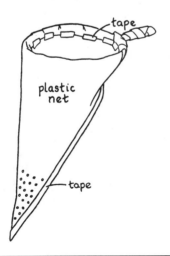

tape

plastic net

tape

7. Holding the handle, turn the insect net sideways and sweep its open end through the air above the leaves of a tree or bush.

8. When you have caught an insect in the net, squeeze the net closed near the opening to keep the insect from escaping.

9. Ask your helper to hold the vegetable bag open. Hold the net over the bag and push the net through the hoop and into the bag, turning the net inside out until you see the insect enter the bag.

10. Have your helper seal the bag as soon as you remove the net.

11. Identify the insect using the field guide. *NOTE: Keep the bag out of direct sunlight and after 60 minutes or less, release the insect where you found it.*

Results

The net enables you to catch and identify different flying insects.

Why?

As you hold the handle and move the net, insects sitting on the leaves take flight. The air and any insect in front of the net are swept inside the net. The holes in the plastic bag allow air to pass through, so you can keep the insect for a short period of time while you identify it. Direct sunlight could cause the inside of the bag to get too hot and injure or kill the insect.

You should be able to identify the insects you catch using the field guide. Insects and all **organisms** (living things) are **classified**, or grouped, according to their similarities. The largest classifications into which organisms are grouped are **kingdoms**. Kingdoms are divided into smaller groups called **phyla**. Each phylum is divided into **classes**, classes are divided into **orders**, orders into **families**, families into **genera**, and genera into species. A **species** is a group of organisms that are the same kind and can produce offspring. **Insects** belong to the Animal Kingdom, the phylum **Arthropoda**, and the class **Insecta**.

To use a field guide to identify an insect, you first determine the insect's order. (Most field guides have a key or guide to insect orders.) Once you have determined the order, look in the guide for the descriptions of insects in that order. You should then be able to find the species or a closely related species of your insect.

LET'S EXPLORE

Do the orders and species of flying insects vary in different **habitats** (physical places where plants or animals live)? Repeat steps 7 through 11 of the experiment, sweeping the net in different habitats, such as grassy fields, forests, deserts, or near a pond. *CAUTION: Only visit a pond or other water habitat with an adult. Protect your skin from insect bites.* **Science Fair Hint:** Have your helper take photos of you using the insect net in different habitats. Display the photos to show how to catch flying insects. When finished, remember to release the insects where you found them.

SHOW TIME!

1. Another way to catch flying or crawling insects is to place a clear plastic cup over the insect, then slip an index card under the cup to cover the mouth of the cup. Keep the card in place and carry the cup to a table

where you can observe and identify the insect. Release the insect where you found it as soon as possible after observing it.

2. Prepare a holding jar to observe insects for several days by adding 3 to 4 twigs to a 1-gallon (4-liter) jar. Fold a paper towel in half four to five times and moisten it with tap water. Place the moist towel and food in the jar. Look in books like *Pet Bugs* by Sally Kneidel (New York: Wiley, 1994) for information on the food and additional materials needed in the jar for specific

insects. Place your insects in the jar and immediately cover the opening with a knee-high stocking.

If necessary, you can drop additional food and another moist towel into the jar by lifting a portion of the stocking. *NOTE: You can use the holding jar to keep insects or spiders from other experiments in this book.*

CHECK IT OUT!

The word *bug* is often used to refer to any insect. But while all bugs are insects, all insects are not true bugs. Find out what a true bug is. How can true bugs be caught?

2

Diggers

PROBLEM

What kinds of insects live in soil?

Materials

trowel
2-quart (2-liter) bowl
ruler
2 sheets of white poster board
colander with small holes
colander with large holes
three 1-quart (1-liter) glass jars
index card
3 knee-high stockings
magnifying lens
insect field guide (See the Appendix.)
sponge (optional)
1 teaspoon (5 ml) tap water (optional)

Procedure

NOTE: Ask an adult for permission to remove the soil samples. If possible, repeat this experiment during different seasons.

1. Use the trowel to remove the **leaf litter** (layers of newly fallen and partially decayed leaves covering the soil) from beneath a tree or bush. Fill the bowl with the soil under the leaf litter. Dig no deeper than 4 inches (10 cm).

2. Lay the poster boards on the ground.

3. Use the trowel to transfer about one-third of the soil from the bowl to the small-holed colander. Gently shake the colander to spread a thin layer of soil over one of the poster boards.

4. Transfer any soil that does not fall through the first colander into the second, large-holed colander. Gently shake the second colander to spread a

thin layer of soil over the second
poster board.

5. Look for insects in the soil layer on
each poster board.

6. Transfer the insects to one of the jars
by holding the edge of the index card
near each insect and allowing it to
crawl onto the card.

7. Cover the jar with a stocking.

8. Repeat steps 3 through 7 until all
insects have been placed in jars.

9. Use the magnifying lens and field
guide to study and identify each
insect. *NOTE: After 60 minutes or less,
replace the soil and insects where you*

found them. If more time is needed to study the insects, fill the jars with the collected soil and add a small piece of sponge moistened with water. If the soil is dry, add 1 teaspoon (5 ml) of water. Use colanders to separate insects and soil for observation. Release the insects within 3 to 4 days.

Results

You find different kinds of insects.

Why?

Many insects live on and in soil. You can find different active adult insects, such as beetles, earwigs, mole crickets, and ants, all year long in regions with mild winters. You will find the largest number of adult insects during warm weather. While some adult insects are active during the winter, most insects are **dormant** (in an inactive state) during the cold season.

LET'S EXPLORE

Would soil from different locations contain different kinds of insects? Repeat the experiment, taking soil samples from different locations, such as an open area (not covered by a tree or bush), an area near a building, or a garden. Remember to replace the insects where you found them when finished. **Science Fair Hint:** Make and display diagrams of each insect found.

SHOW TIME!

1a. Create a "bug catcher" to observe insects found on the surface of soil. Do this by cutting off the top 4 inches (10 cm) of a 2-liter plastic soda bottle. Place half of an over-ripe banana in the bottom part of the bottle. Insert the top part of the bottle backward into the bottom part. Lay the bug catcher on its side on the soil as shown for 6 to 8 hours.

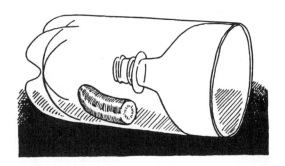

Observe the bug catcher as often as possible during the 6 to 8 hours. Use a field guide to identify the insects that enter the bug catcher. At the end of the experiment, release insects where you found them.

b. Study the insects on the soil in different locations by making several bug catchers and placing them in different areas.

2. Prepare and display an identification guide for the insects you find. Make an information page for each insect as shown. Take a photo or draw a diagram of the insect and place it on the information page.

Design a system for organizing the guide. You may want to put all insects of the same order together. Once the guide is organized, number the pages and prepare a table of contents. Prepare a title page, such as "Instant Guide to Central Texas Insects." Protect the pages of your guide by placing them in see-through plastic sheet protectors and store them in a ringed binder. You can use the binder as part of a project display.

Order: Orthoptera
Family: Blattidae
Common Name: American cockroach

Description: Flat, oval, reddish-brown body with long, slender antennae about 1½ in.(3.75cm) long, with wings covering its thorax and abdomen.
Location: Found near the base of a tree.
Miscellaneous: One of the oldest insect groups. Scavengers, feeding on garbage or human food, which they contaminate with their waste.

CHECK IT OUT!

June beetles are a common beetle usually first seen in June. During the warm weather, they spend their days buried a few inches (cm) under the soil and come out at night to eat leaves, to mate, and to lay eggs in the soil. Find out more about June beetles and other insects that are dependent on soil, such as cicadas. For information about trapping beetles, see page 64 of *Looking at Insects* by David Suzuki (New York: Wiley, 1992).

3

Jointed

PROBLEM

What are the main external identifying features of adult insects?

Materials

pencil
1-quart (1-liter) resealable plastic bag
cricket (Catch it by following the
    instructions below or purchase one
    from a pet store or catalog supplier.
    See the Appendix.)
10-ounce (300-ml) clear plastic cup
4-by-6-inch (10-by-15 cm) index card
magnifying lens
helper

Procedure

*NOTE: If you caught or purchased the
cricket, you may release it outdoors when
finished or move the cricket from the bag to
a holding jar until needed for the next
experiment. (See Chapter 1, page 7, for
instructions on preparing a holding jar.)
Feed the cricket any kind of fruit, vegetables, or bread.*

1. Use the point of the pencil to make 15 to 20 small airholes through both layers of the top half of the bag.

2. To catch the cricket, place the cup over it, then slip the index card under the cup to cover the mouth of the cup.

3. Ask your helper to hold the bag open. Hold the cup and card over the bag.

4. Slowly slide the card away so the cricket drops into the bag. Have the helper quickly seal the bag.

5. With your hand, *gently* press the bag against the cricket and feel the texture of the cricket's body.

6. Hold the cricket still by continuing to gently press the bag against its body. Use the magnifying lens to study the cricket's body and legs.

Results

The cricket has three distinct body parts and three pairs of legs. Its legs and body are covered with a hard outer covering.

Why?

The cricket, like all adult insects, has a body made up of three main parts in this order: **head**, **thorax**, and **abdomen**. Adult insects also have three pairs of

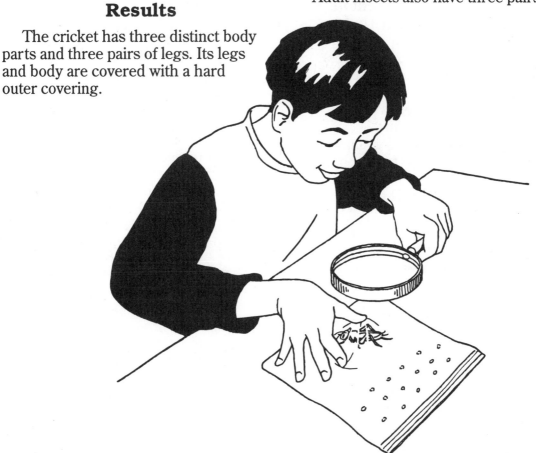

jointed (parts that fit together) legs attached to the thorax. All three body parts and all six legs have a jointed outer covering called an **exoskeleton**. This covering is made mostly of a relatively hard but flexible material called **chitin**. The exoskeleton provides support and protection for the insect's body. The **cerci** (pair of feelerlike or clasplike structures), **ovipositor** (female egg-laying structure), eyes, and **antennae** (sensory parts of the head) are also identifying features.

Insects belong to the phylum Arthropoda. All animals in this group are called **arthropods**. All adult arthropods have jointed legs and segmented bodies covered by an exoskeleton. They are all **invertebrates**, meaning they do not have a backbone. Insects are the largest group of arthropods. The four other arthropod groups are **arachnids** (spiders),

crustaceans (crabs, shrimps, lobsters, and wood lice), **millipedes** (wormlike organisms having two pairs of legs per body segment), and **centipedes** (worm-like organisms having one pair of legs per body segment). The two main features that distinguish the bodies of insects from the bodies of other arthropods are three body parts and three pairs of legs. This is called the 3 + 3 rule.

LET'S EXPLORE

Repeat the original experiment to catch other insects, such as grasshoppers or praying mantises. Observe the body parts of these insects. When finished, release the insects where you found them. **Science Fair Hint:** Prepare a display comparing the similarities and differences of body parts. *CAUTION: Use insect field guides to identify the insects you plan to catch. Do not touch any insect unless you are sure it is harmless. If in doubt, do not touch.*

SHOW TIME!

1. Insecta is the largest class of arthropods. In fact, insects outnumber all other animals on the earth! Find out

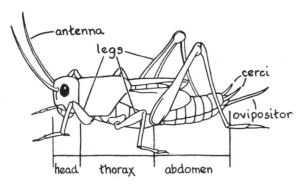

more about the number of insects and other arthropod classes. Prepare and display a pie chart similar to the one shown, comparing the size of each class.

2. **Spiders** are arthropods in the Arachnida class. See Chapter 19, "Relatives," and use books on spiders to find out the name and function of each body part of spiders. Use the procedure in the original experiment to catch a jumping spider (Salticidae) and a garden spider (Araneidae). *CAUTION: Use the spider books to be sure to identify a jumping and a garden spider.* Place the spiders in separate resealable plastic bags.

Lay the bags on a table and use a magnifying lens to study the outer features of these different spiders close-up. Notice the number of body parts including legs. Take photographs of the spiders and/or collect pictures from books. Prepare a display using the photos or pictures to show different arachnids and compare their body parts. In 60 minutes or less, return the spiders to the areas where you found them.

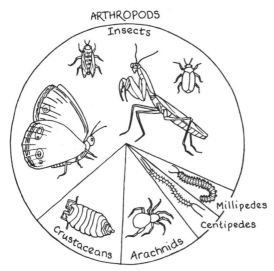

ARTHROPODS
Insects
Millipedes
Centipedes
Crustaceans
Arachnids

CHECK IT OUT!

1. Two groups of arthropods, centipedes and millipedes, are wormlike in appearance. *Centipede* means 100 legs and *millipede* means 1,000 legs. Find out more about these arthropods. Do they really have that many legs? How do their bodies compare to those of other arthropods?

2. Find out more about the group of arthropods called crustaceans. How do the bodies of crustaceans compare to those of other arthropods?

3-D

PROBLEM

How can you make a model of an adult insect's three main body parts?

Materials

4-ounce (113-g) stick of clay
sheet of paper
ruler
table knife
round toothpick
pencil
4-by-8-inch (10-by-20 cm) unruled
  index card

Procedure

1. Lay the clay on the paper. Roll it into a tube 6 inches (15 cm) long.

2. Use the knife to cut the clay roll into three pieces: 1 inch (2.5 cm), 2 inches (5 cm), and 3 inches (7.5 cm) long.

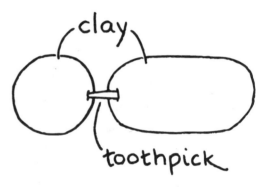

3. Round the end of each piece of clay.

4. Break the toothpick in half. Use one half of the toothpick to connect the 1-inch (2.5-cm) piece of clay to the 2-inch (5-cm) piece. Push the two clay pieces together so they touch.

5. Use the remaining half of the toothpick to connect the 3-inch (7.5-cm) piece of clay to the free end of the

2-inch (5-cm) piece. Push the clay pieces together as before.

6. Lay the connected clay on the paper and mold into the shape of an insect's body as shown in the diagram.

7. Use the point of the pencil to carve two shallow grooves around the middle clay section, dividing it into three parts. Carve nine shallow grooves around the large end section, dividing it into ten parts.

8. Place the clay model on the index card and label the parts as shown.

Results

You have made a three-dimensional model of an insect's main body parts.

Why?

An adult insect's body is divided into three main body parts: the head, the thorax, and the abdomen. The head is the front part. The thorax is the middle part, which is divided into three smaller segments. The abdomen is the rear part, which is divided into ten or fewer smaller segments. Every insect has the same three body parts, with the abdomen and thorax divided into 13 or fewer segments.

LET'S EXPLORE

1a. Eyes, **mouthparts** (body parts used to gather and eat food), and antennae (long, thin, movable body parts used to smell, feel, and some-

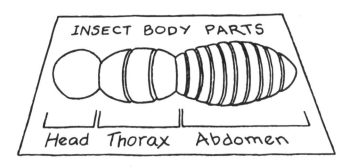

times to hear) are located on the insect's head. Find out about the number, size, and exact location of these parts. Repeat the activity to prepare the head and thorax, but do not connect them. Set the thorax aside for the following activities.

Design ways to make models of the eyes, mouthparts, and antennae on the clay head, such as by using pipe cleaners for antennae and balls of clay for eyes. Insert differently colored toothpicks at each head part location and make a color-keyed legend of the toothpicks. **Science Fair Hint:** Display the head model on a separate index card with labels and legends.

b. One pair of jointed (consisting of different parts that fit together) legs is attached to each of the three sections of an insect's thorax, one on each side. Each leg has four main parts, from the **coxa** connected to the body, to the **femur**, **tibia**, and **tarsus** at the outermost end of the leg. Observe an insect to determine the approximate length of each leg segment. Use pipe

cleaners to represent legs. Attach the legs to the thorax and bend the pipe cleaners to show each leg segment.

c. Insect wings, when present, are in pairs. If only one pair is present, it is attached to the middle thorax segment. But most insects have two pairs of wings. The second pair is attached to the third thorax segment. Find out the length of insect wings and add wing models to the clay thorax. Make wing models by cutting them from waxed paper. Tape a toothpick to one end of each wing and insert the toothpicks in the clay.

SHOW TIME!

Most adult insects have wings. Insect wings vary in number, size, shape, texture, **veins** (framework of thickened ridges), and position at which they are held at rest. The number and arrangement of veins are used to identify insects. Some insects, such as flies, have two wings. Most winged adult insects, like butterflies, moths, dragonflies, wasps,

and bees, have four wings. Most insect wings are **membranous** (resembling a thin, flexible sheet of tissue paper) and may have tiny hairs or scales. Some insects, such as beetles, have thick, leathery, or even hard front wings.

Use a field guide to find out more about insect wings and design different models. Display the models with drawings or pictures of the insect that has each wing type. Use waxed paper for transparent wings. Draw the veins on these wings with a permanent marker. Construction paper can be used to form thick wings. See Chapter 10, "Lifters," for information about scaled butterfly wings.

CHECK IT OUT!

Insects have a heart and blood, but no blood vessels. Find out more about insects' internal body parts. How does their blood circulate? How can models of an insect's internal body parts be made?

5

Break Out

Problem

What happens to the exoskeleton of a growing insect?

Materials

12-inch (30-cm) round balloon
spring-type clothespin
1 tablespoon (15 ml) school glue
1 tablespoon (15 ml) tap water
small bowl
spoon
35 to 40 newspaper strips, each about
    2 × 4 inches (5 × 10 cm)

Procedure

1. Blow up the balloon to about the size of a grapefruit.

2. Twist the end closed and secure it with the clothespin.

3. Put the glue and water in the bowl and mix them by stirring with the spoon.

4. Dip a newspaper strip in the glue mixture and stick the strip on the balloon.

5. Repeat this with a second paper strip, placing it on the balloon so that it overlaps half of the first paper strip.

6. Continue adding strips, overlapping each one until most of the balloon is covered with paper. Leave a narrow strip around the balloon uncovered.

7. Wait an hour or so until the paper dries.

8. Once the paper is dry, remove the clothespin without letting the air out. Gently blow into the balloon, making it slightly larger.

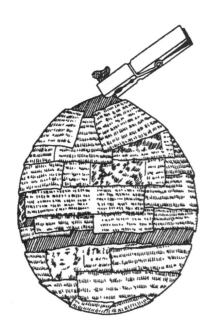

Results

A firm paper shell covers the balloon. When you blow up the balloon even more, the uncovered section of the paper shell separates.

Why?

The balloon and hard paper shell represent an insect during a growing stage. The body of the growing insect is covered by an exoskeleton. This exoskeleton does not grow with the insect. As the rest of the insect's body grows, the exoskeleton starts to become too small. A new exoskeleton begins to form under the old one.

When the old exoskeleton becomes too small for the growing insect, blood and sometimes air or water inside the insect is forced into the thorax by the **contraction** (squeezing together) of muscles in the abdomen. This splits the exoskeleton, usually along the middle of the back side, and the insect crawls out. This process of shedding the exoskeleton is called **molting**. Most insects molt four to eight times during their lives, but they typically do not molt or continue to grow in size once they reach the adult stage.

LET'S EXPLORE

When the insect first crawls out of its old exoskeleton, its new exoskeleton is still moist and flexible like the wet paper strips on the balloon. The insect gulps in air or water to expand the flexible exoskeleton before it dries and hardens like the paper strips. The dried, stretched exoskeleton provides growing space until the next molt.

Demonstrate the stretching of an insect's exoskeleton by repeating the experiment. While the glue is still wet, stand in front of a mirror and observe the paper covering as you slightly blow up the balloon. While the exoskeleton model is enlarged, twist the open end of the balloon and secure it with a clothespin. Allow the paper to dry, then let a little air out of the balloon. **Science Fair Hint:** Display diagrams showing the changes in the paper model of an exoskeleton.

SHOW TIME!

Mealworms are **darkling beetles** in a growing stage. Purchase a container of mealworms from a pet store. *NOTE: You will need to plan what to do with your mealworms when you are through experimenting. See page iv (dedication page), "Handling Insects and Spiders."* Spread the contents of the container on a paper towel and look for exoskeletons that have been discarded by molting mealworms.

Sort the mealworms by length, placing them in three piles: short, medium, and long. Use three plastic containers with lids, such as empty, clean, 4-cup (1.36-kg) margarine containers, to house the three groups of mealworms. Fill each container about half full with cornmeal. Place a potato slice and mealworms on the surface of the cornmeal. Fold a paper towel in half twice and place it over the potato slice, mealworms, and cornmeal. Secure the lids, then make 10 to 15 airholes in each lid with the point of a pencil. Label the containers SMALL, MEDIUM, and LARGE.

Place the containers on a tray. Set the tray in an area at room temperature and out of direct light. Observe the contents of each container every 2 to 3 days for 3 to 4 weeks. Measure and record the average length of the mealworms in each container. Record changes in the length of the mealworms and the number of exoskeletons you find. Observe the width of the mealworms and make note of any changes. *NOTE: Remove the old potato slice and add a new one each week.*

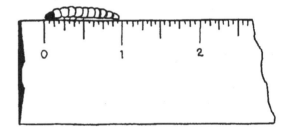

CHECK IT OUT!

Insects produce *hormones*, which are chemicals that control molting and other processes. The hormone that controls molting in immature insects is called *ecdysone*. For more information about molting hormones, see pages 29–33 of *Entomology* by H. Steven Dashefsky (New York: TAB Books, 1994). What does the juvenile hormone control?

6

Wigglers

PROBLEM

What are the body parts of a mealworm?

Materials

2 cups (500 ml) cornmeal
4-cup (1-liter) or larger plastic container (such as empty margarine container)
slice of potato
small container of mealworms (available at pet stores)
paper towel
pencil
index card
desk lamp (optional)
magnifying lens
pencil
paper

Procedure

NOTE: At the end of this experiment, keep the remaining mealworms for the rest of the experiments in this chapter. You will need to plan what to do with the mealworms when you are through experimenting. See page iv (dedication page), "Handling Insects and Spiders."

1. Prepare housing for the mealworms.
- Pour the cornmeal into the plastic container.
- Place the potato slice and mealworms on the surface of the cornmeal.
- Fold the paper towel in half twice and place it over the potato slice, mealworms, and cornmeal.
- Secure the lid and make 10 to 15 airholes in the lid with the point of the pencil.

2. Remove the lid and paper towel. Use the end of the index card to pick up one mealworm.

3. Place the card on a flat surface under the lamp or near a window.

4. Use the magnifying lens to examine the mealworm. Record your observations by drawing and labeling parts of the mealworm. Include head, antennae, legs, and body segments.

5. Repeat steps 2 through 4, using 4 or more mealworms.

6. When you are finished, return the mealworms and paper towel to the container. Secure the lid.

Results

The mealworm has a head and a wormlike, segmented body. The head has visible mouthparts and two short antennae. There are three pairs of legs attached to the body, one pair on each of the first three body segments after the head. The body is covered with a firm outer skin.

Why?

Mealworms do not have the same identifying features as adult insects (three main body parts and three pairs of legs). This is because mealworms are not adult insects. Mealworms are **larvae**, which are immature insects that differ greatly from the adult. Mealworms develop into adult insects called darkling beetles.

Mealworms have a well-developed head with mouthparts and short antennae. The first three segments behind the head are the thorax and the remaining segments are the abdomen. These two areas are more clearly separated in the adult stage. The mealworms have six legs, one pair attached to each thorax segment. They also have an exoskeleton.

Mealworms, like all larvae, grow through a series of molts as they develop. During molts, they shed their exoskeletons. The stages between molts are called **instars**. The last molt of the **larval stage** (active, feeding stage) results in the formation of a **pupa**, a non-feeding insect in the resting stage, or **pupal stage**. Next is the adult stage.

LET'S EXPLORE

Observe and compare the instars of the mealworms. Select 10 or more of the smallest mealworms and prepare a housing container as in the experiment. Measure the larvae and observe them

LARVAL INSTARS

with a magnifying lens every 1 to 2 days until the larvae **pupate** (form a pupa). This may take a few days to weeks, depending on how close your purchased larvae are to the pupal stage. (The pupae are inactive and look like pale mummies.) **Science Fair Hint:** Make diagrams of the instars and use the drawings as part of a project display. *NOTE: Keep the pupae for other experiments.*

SHOW TIME!

1. How do the bodies of the pupal and larval stages of the darkling beetle compare? Use the magnifying lens to study several pupae from the previous experiment.

2a. Using a shoe box and a flashlight, test the response of mealworms to light. Cut a hole in one end of the lid of the shoe box. Make the hole slightly smaller than a flashlight's lens. Place 5 to 10 mealworms in the shoe box beneath the hole. Turn the flashlight on and stand it lens down over the hole. Leave the box undisturbed for 1 hour. Then remove the lid and observe the position of the mealworms.

b. How do darkling beetle pupae respond to light? Repeat the previous experiment, using 5 or more pupae. Observe the pupae with a magnifying lens before and after placing them under the light. Look for any signs of motion.

CHECK IT OUT!

Some larvae have *prolegs*, which are fleshy legs attached to the abdominal region. Find out more about the body structures of larvae.

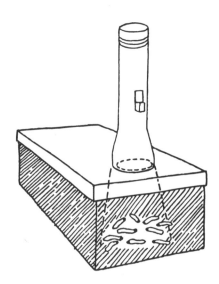

7

Changers

PROBLEM

What are the stages of development of a darkling beetle?

Materials

3 cups (750 ml) cornmeal
4-cup (1-liter) or larger plastic container (such as an empty margarine container)
slice of potato
small container of mealworms (available at pet stores)
paper towel
pencil
paper

PROCEDURE

NOTE: At the end of this experiment, keep the adult beetles for the next experiment. You will need to plan what to do with the beetles and mealworms used in the experiments in this chapter. See page iv (dedication page), "Handling Insects and Spiders."

1. Prepare housing for the mealworms.
   - Pour the cornmeal into the plastic container.
   - Place the potato slice and the mealworms on the surface of the cornmeal.
   - Fold the paper towel in half twice and place it over the potato slice, mealworms, and cornmeal.
   - Secure the lid and make 10 to 15 airholes in the lid with the point of the pencil.

2. Set the mealworm container in a dark area at room temperature.

3. Lift the lid and paper towel daily for 4 to 8 weeks or more. Observe any changes in the mealworms in and/or on the surface of the cornmeal.

Replace the potato slice with a fresh one each week.

Results

You first see different-size mealworms, remains of their exoskeletons, and the pupae, which look like pale mummies. Beetles form about 7 days after the formation of the pupae. (Some pupae may be present when you purchase the container of mealworms, in which case beetles can form in a short time.)

Why?

Darkling beetles, like many insects, develop in several distinct stages. The adult beetles lay eggs in grain. The larvae (mealworms) develop from the eggs. The developing mealworms molt, which means they shed their exoskeletons several times as they grow. Their last molt reveals mummy-looking pupae.

The pupal stage is the resting stage of development. The pupae appear inactive and may even look dead. But there are many changes going on within the bodies of the pupae. When the adult beetles emerge from the pupae, they are soft and pale, but quickly harden and turn dark.

This four-stage process of insect development from **egg** (first stage) to larva to pupa to adult is called **complete metamorphosis**. Ants, fleas, flies, and ladybugs are other insects that develop by complete metamorphosis.

LET'S EXPLORE

At room temperature, it can take about 4 months or more for darkling beetles to go through the four stages of complete metamorphosis from egg to adult. Determine for yourself the exact time required for each stage of a darkling beetle's complete metamorphosis at room temperature. Prepare 3 small housing containers about half the size of the one in the original experiment. Label them A, B, and C. Place 12 or more adult beetles in container A. Record the date the beetles are placed in the container.

Place the container where the temperature varies very little, such as in a draft-free area of your home. The beetles will lay eggs in the cornmeal, but they may be too small to be seen. Look for the first formation of larvae, record the date of discovery, and carefully transfer the larvae to container B. Then, continue to observe container B for the formation of pupae. When pupae are observed, record the date and transfer them to container C. Observe only container C until beetles form. Use previously made plans to handle the contents of containers A, B, and C at the end of the experiment. Take photos and/or make diagrams of each stage

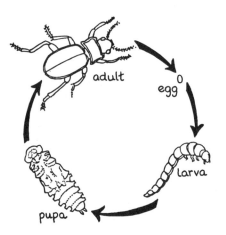

of development and display them to represent the results.

SHOW TIME!

1. Design an experiment to determine if temperature affects the length of time needed for complete metamorphosis.

2. Butterflies and moths also develop by complete metamorphosis. Observe the metamorphosis of butterflies and moths by observing **caterpillars**, the larval stage of butterfly and moth development. See insect field guides for information about where to find caterpillars and how to identify them, or purchase caterpillars from a catalog supplier. (See the Appendix.) *CAUTION: Some caterpillars have spines that sting. Do not touch any caterpillar unless you are sure it is harmless.*

Place the caterpillars in a holding jar with stems and leaves from the plant on which you found them. Supply the caterpillars daily with fresh leaves to eat from these same plants. Cover the top of the jar with a knee-high stocking. Caterpillars produce a lot of body waste, which must be dumped out frequently.

Watch each stage of development carefully. Observe the eating habits and movements of the caterpillars during each instar, or stage between molts. Take photos of growth stages to display. Release the adult butterfly or moth outside as soon as possible after it emerges.

CHECK IT OUT!

Monarch butterflies are one of the few insects that *migrate* (move from one region to another when the seasons change). Find out more about the migration and life cycle of monarch butterflies.

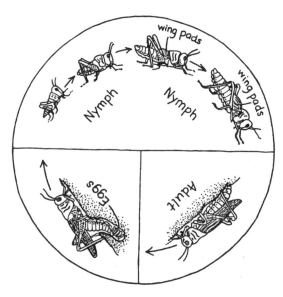

8

Gradual

PROBLEM

How can you make a model showing the stages of a grasshopper's development?

Materials

drawing compass
2 file folders
scissors
pencil
ruler
paper brad
adult helper

Procedure

1. Use the compass to draw an 8-inch (20-cm) circle on one of the folders. Cut out the circle.

2. Use the pencil and ruler to draw a line through the center of the circle, dividing the circle in half. On one of the halves, draw a second line dividing it in half.

3. In each section, draw and label the stages of development of the grasshopper as shown in the diagram.

4. Cut across the open edge of the second folder so that the tab is removed and the two edges are even.

5. Center the circle inside the folder with about 1 inch (2.5 cm) of the circle above the open edge of the folder.

6. Ask an adult to use the point of the compass to make a hole through the center of the circle and both layers of the folder.

7. Insert the paper brad through the holes so that the circle turns like a wheel.

8. Label the folder INCOMPLETE METAMOR-PHOSIS, then cut out a section of the folder as shown.

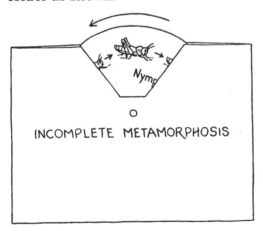

9. Set the wheel so that the egg stage is visible, then turn the wheel counterclockwise.

Results

As the wheel turns, it reveals the three different stages of grasshopper development.

Why?

You have made a model of the stages of grasshopper development. Grasshoppers do not develop by complete metamorphosis. Instead of four stages of development, insects like grasshoppers develop in three stages. The young insects look very much like the adults, and there is no pupal stage. This type of insect development is called **gradual** or **incomplete metamorphosis**.

The three stages of gradual metamorphosis are the egg, nymph, and adult. The **nymph** is the young insect. It closely resembles the adult, but is smaller and wingless. Nymphs grow through a series of molts. As nymphs of grasshoppers and nymphs of other winged adult insects grow, small winglike growths called **wing pads** appear. The wing pads increase in size only slightly up to the last molt. After the last molt, the adult appears with wings expanded to their full size.

LET'S EXPLORE

How different are gradual and complete metamorphoses? Use insect field guides or biology texts to find diagrams of each stage of complete metamorphosis of an insect, such as a butterfly. Repeat the experiment to make a model of complete metamorphosis. **Science Fair Hint:** Secure the two models to your display and turn the wheels at the same time to compare the stages of the two types of metamorphosis.

SHOW TIME!

Catch or purchase and raise insect nymphs, such as praying mantis nymphs. Look for small versions of the adult mantis. Catch them with your hand and place them in a holding jar with twigs on which they can climb. Leave the bottom of the jar bare and cover the mouth of the jar with a knee-high stocking. Feed your young mantises live insects, such as crickets, which can be caught or purchased at a pet store.

Add a few drops of water or mist the jar with water daily. Observe the nymphs daily or as often as possible. Look for body changes, such as size or presence of wing pads. Watch for signs of molting. Keep a written record of your observations and include diagrams. Use the diagrams to make a display poster of gradual metamorphosis. When you are through experimenting, remember to release all insects where you found them. See page iv (dedication page) for information on releasing purchased insects. For more information about catching and raising praying mantises and other insects that develop by gradual metamorphosis, see *Pet Bugs* by Sally Kneidel (New York: Wiley, 1994).

CHECK IT OUT!

All insects develop from eggs. Most develop from eggs that have been laid. But a few, such as aphids, develop from eggs that stay in the body of the female. Find out more about the gradual metamorphosis of aphids. What is parthenogenesis?

9

Bug-Eyed

PROBLEM

What kind of eyes do grasshoppers have?

Materials

grasshopper (Catch it by following the
instructions below or purchase one
from a catalog supplier. See the
Appendix.)
insect net from Chapter 1
1-quart (1-liter) jar
knee-high stocking
magnifying lens

Procedure

*CAUTION: Grasshoppers may bite, so do
not hold one with your bare hands.*

1. Catch a grasshopper by sweeping the
insect net through high grass.

2. Transfer the grasshopper to the jar
and cover the jar's mouth with the
stocking.

3. Use the magnifying lens to study the
head of the grasshopper, looking spe-
cifically for the eyes shown in the diagram.

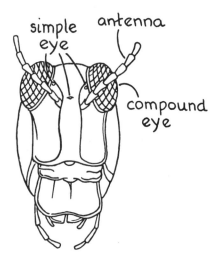

Results

The grasshopper has two large eyes, one on each side of its head. It has three small eyes that look like little bumps between the two large eyes.

Why?

The grasshopper, like most adult insects, has two large eyes called **compound eyes**, one on each side of its head. These eyes are made up of thousands of separate units called **ommatidia**. At the surface of each ommatidium is a lens called a **facet**. (A **lens** is the part of the eye that focuses light rays.) The ommatidia are grouped together so that the facets form a honeycomb pattern. Each ommatidium receives a small bit of light from the total scene that the insect sees. These separate images are sent to the brain, where they are combined to form the whole picture.

Many adult insects also have smaller eyes called **ocelli**, or simple eyes. The grasshopper has three **simple eyes**, all located between its compound eyes. Simple eyes do not have ommatidia and have only one facet. They can see the difference between light and dark, but cannot see images.

LET'S EXPLORE

Are the locations of the compound and simple eyes the same for all adult insects? Repeat the experiment, studying the eyes of other insects, such as crickets or praying mantises. You can safely catch these insects with your hands. Crickets can also be purchased at pet stores. **Science Fair Hint:** Make diagrams for a display showing the position and size of the eyes of different insects.

SHOW TIME!

1. Scientists do not know what an insect actually sees. To get an idea of what it might be like to receive images from the multiple facets of a compound eye, cut a toilet-tissue tube so that it opens. Stand 24 flexible drinking straws together on a flat surface, flexible sections up. Wrap the toilet-tissue tube around the flexible parts of the straws. Secure the tube with tape.

   Hold the free end of the tube near, but not touching, your eye. Close one eye and look through the tube with your open eye. Look at stationary and moving objects, such as the blades of a rotating ceiling fan. Display the eye model along with diagrams of compound eyes and ommatidia found in insect books, such as *Insect* by Lawrence Mound (New York: Eyewitness Books, Dorling Kindersley/Knopf, 1990, pages 14–15).

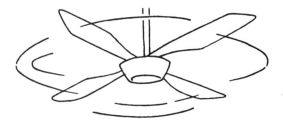

2. Some insects can distinguish colors. Determine whether insects are more attracted to certain colors. Make a sugar-water solution by mixing 1 tablespoon (15 ml) of table sugar with 1 cup (250 ml) of tap water. This will attract insects that feed on **nectar** (a sugary liquid produced by many flowers at the base of their petals). Fill small, equal-size bowls or jar lids half full with the sugar-water solution.

Cut 6-inch (15-cm) circles from differently colored poster board, such as yellow, orange, red, blue, green, and black. Set these circles on a table or on the ground outdoors. Evenly distribute the circles and leave about 4 to 6 inches (10 to 15 cm) of space between them. Place one sugar-water container on each circle. Stand at a distance of about 10 feet (3 m) and use binoculars to observe the con-

tainers periodically for at least 30 minutes. Make note of the number of insects visiting each container. Make observations as often as possible every day for 3 to 4 days. Replace the sugar water each day. Use insect field guides to identify the insects visiting the containers.

CHECK IT OUT!

Insects cannot move or focus any of their eyes. How does the position of the compound eyes affect the direction that insects can see? Are insects nearsighted or farsighted? Do they have binocular vision?

Lifters

PROBLEM

How do winged insects fly?

Materials

scissors
ruler
tissue paper

Procedure

1. Cut a 2-by-10-inch (5-by-25-cm) strip from the paper.

2. Hold one end of the strip against your chin, just below your bottom lip.

3. Blow hard just above the top of the strip. Observe the movement of the strip.

Results

The paper strip lifts up.

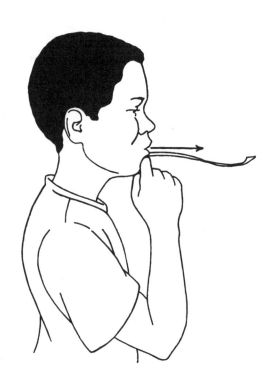

Why?

When you blow above the top of the paper strip, the air above the strip moves faster than the air below it. When any fluid, such as air, flows across a surface, its **pressure** (force acting upon a surface) decreases as its speed increases. (This law of nature is called **Bernoulli's principle**.) Thus, because the air above the paper strip is moving faster than the air below it, the air pressure above the paper strip is less than the air pressure below the strip. This difference in air pressure causes the strip to lift.

Similarly, when an insect flies, the shape and movement of its wings draw air from above and in front of the insect. This air moves faster, which results in less air pressure above and in front of the insect than below and behind it. The difference in air pressure causes the insect to lift and move forward.

LET'S EXPLORE

1. Butterflies and moths have tiny, light-weight, flattened hairs called **scales** covering their wings. Each scale has a peg that fits into the wing. Make a model to determine if scales affect the lift of the wings. Repeat the experiment covering part of the paper strip with scales. Use colored, round, ¾-inch (1.88-cm) diameter self-stick labels for scales. Your paper scales are heavier than butterfly or moth scales, so yours will only cover part of the model wing.

   Start about 4 inches (10 cm) from one end of the paper strip. Stick a row of 3 labels across the paper, placing the first label next to the left side of the paper strip. Start the next row slightly above the first, with the first label next to the right side of the paper strip as shown. Repeat the procedure, making two more rows. Cut off the parts of the labels that overlap the edges. **Science Fair Hint:** Use the wing models as part of a project display.

2. The scales on a butterfly or moth's wing can be rubbed off or damaged when something touches the wing. The loss of the scales does not kill the insect. However, it can affect the air-flow across the wings, which in turn can affect the ability of the insect to control how it flies.

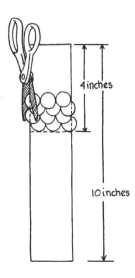

Demonstrate in an exaggerated way how damaged scales affect the airflow across the wing, using the strip from the previous experiment. Bend up 2 to 3 of the labels on different rows of the paper strip. Then repeat steps 2 and 3 of the original experiment. Remember, your paper scales are much larger than real insect scales and affect the airflow more than would the tiny scales on a butterfly or moth's wing.

Science Fair Hint: Have a helper take photos while you blow across the wings. Use the photos to represent the results of these experiments.

SHOW TIME!

1. Adult beetles have a front pair of thick, leathery, or hard wings. When the beetle is resting, these wings come together. They form a line that runs straight down the middle of the back and cover the thin, papery back wings.

Catch different beetles and observe the structure of their wings. Make note of the different textures of the front wings. Try to see how the front and back wings move when the beetle is preparing to fly. In warm months, catch June beetles using your hands or the cup-and-card method from Chapter 1, "Catchers." For information for catching ladybird beetles and Japanese beetles, see pages 18–19 and 90–92 of *Pet Bugs* by Sally Kneidel (New York: Wiley, 1994).

Use insect field guides and books to find out more about the wings of beetles. Make a display poster of drawings or photos of different beetles to show how their front wings differ. Remember to return the insects where you found them when you are finished experimenting.

2. In what positions do resting insects hold their wings? Discover the answer by observing the position of as many winged insects at rest as possible. Use binoculars to observe the insects without disturbing them. Check insect field guides and books to discover the most common position of the wings of resting insects.

CHECK IT OUT!

Insects are one of the few animals that can fly. Many insects are much more skilled at flying than birds—only hummingbirds approach insects' ability to move around during flight. Not all flying insects have such flight skills, however. Find out more about the ability of insects to fly. How has flight contributed to the success of insects as a group?

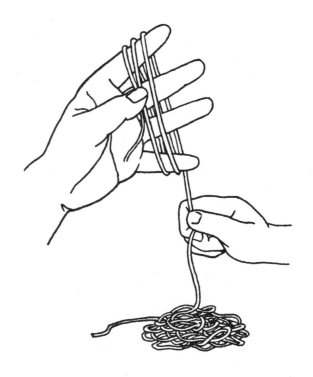

Clingers

PROBLEM

How do fleas hold on to their hosts?

Materials

scissors
ruler
10 feet (3 m) of rug yarn
masking tape
4-by-8-inch (10-by-20-cm) piece of
    cardboard
medium-tooth comb

Procedure

1. Cut a 6-inch (15-cm) piece from one
end of the yarn and set it aside.

2. Spread the fingers of one hand apart
and wrap the remaining yarn around
your fingers.

3. Remove the loop of yarn from your
hand.

4. Tie the strands together with the small, 6-inch (15-cm) piece of yarn.

5. Tape the ends of the small piece of yarn to the center of one short end of the cardboard.

6. Cut the bottom of the loop to form straight pieces of yarn.

7. Lay the cardboard on a table.

8. Holding the taped end of the yarn, push the teeth of the comb into the yarn. Try to comb the yarn.

Results

The comb sticks in the yarn.

Why?

The teeth of the comb are not spaced apart widely enough to easily pass through the yarn.

A flea has spiny structures on its head similar to the teeth of the comb. Like the teeth of the comb, the flea's spiny head sticks in the thick hair or fur of animals, keeping the flea from falling off the animal.

LET'S EXPLORE

1. Does the type of fur affect a flea's holding power? Repeat the experiment, using crochet thread to represent fine (thin) fur.

2. How are the spines in a flea's head spaced if it is a species that lives on an animal with fine fur? Use combs with differently spaced teeth. Which type of comb sticks in the crochet thread?

Science Fair Hint: Display the thick and fine fur models along with the types of combs that stick in each.

SHOW TIME!

Insects do not have feet as you do. Instead, the legs of most adult insects end in a pair of claws, usually with one or more padlike structures between them. The pads between the claws of flies are covered with moist hairs that allow them to walk on the ceiling or on slippery surfaces. The moist hairs on the pads wet the ceiling or surface, and then stick to the wet surface.

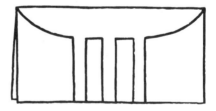

Demonstrate this type of holding power by making a paper model of this type of insect leg. Cut a 2-inch (5-cm)

square from a piece of typing paper and fold it in half. Use the pattern shown to draw half of an insect on the paper. Cut out the insect, cutting through both layers of paper. Open the paper, bend the legs down, then bend the end of the paper legs to form the insect's "feet."

Wet the feet with water. Hold a saucer upright and touch the wet feet to the saucer's outside bottom. Release the paper. The paper feet should stick to the saucer. Thus, the insect hangs upside down from the saucer.

CHECK IT OUT!

Many insects, such as the praying mantis, have spines on their front legs. They use these spines to grab and hold prey. Find out more about how insects cling and hold onto objects. How do head lice cling to hair?

12

Juicy

PROBLEM

How do flies eat?

Materials

eyedropper
jar of sweet-potato baby food
craft stick
masking tape
pen

Procedure

1. Place the tip of the eyedropper just below the surface of the potatoes in the jar. Try to fill the eyedropper with the sweet potatoes. Observe the amount of sweet potatoes that enter the eyedropper, if any.

2. Wash the eyedropper and allow it to dry.

3. Collect as much saliva in your mouth as possible, put the saliva on the craft stick, and transfer the saliva to the surface of the potatoes in the jar. Close the jar.

4. Place a piece of tape across the lid and down the sides of the jar. Label the tape DO NOT EAT.

5. Place the jar in the refrigerator and leave it undisturbed for 1 day.

6. After 24 hours, remove the jar from the refrigerator and repeat step 1.

Results

On your first try, you can draw little or no potatoes into the eyedropper. After the saliva has been in the jar for 24 hours, the potatoes at the surface are liquid. You can then easily draw them into the eyedropper.

Why?

Human saliva, like the saliva of flies and many other insects, contains a chemical called **amylase**. Amylase breaks down **starch**, a complex chemical found in many foods, into less complex chemicals. When humans eat food containing starch, amylase in the saliva begins to **digest** (break down into an absorbable form) the starch in the food. In the experiment, the amylase in your saliva digested the potatoes, turning them to liquid. The

digesting process started as soon as the saliva touched the food, but it took 24 hours for enough liquid to form for you to be able to draw it into the eyedropper.

As you did in the experiment, flies drop saliva on the food they plan to eat. The amylase in the fly saliva quickly begins to digest the starch in the food. The fly dabs at the liquefied food with the end of its tubelike mouthpart called a **proboscis**. The spongy end of the proboscis soaks up the liquid. The liquid food then moves through the proboscis into the insect's digestive system, where the food is further broken down and the nourishing parts are absorbed by the body.

LET'S EXPLORE

Potatoes, rice, and pasta are all starchy foods. Can amylase in fly saliva dissolve nonstarchy foods? Repeat the experiment using jars of nonstarchy foods, such as chicken, meat, or spinach.

SHOW TIME!

1. Butterflies and moths use the proboscis to reach the sweet, sugary nectar of flowers. The proboscis stays coiled

under the head of the butterfly or moth when not in use. Blood from the insect's body is forced into the proboscis, causing the proboscis to uncoil. When uncoiled, the proboscis is used by the insect to suck up nectar.

Demonstrate the coiling and uncoiling of a proboscis with a party blower. Place the party blower upside down in your mouth so that the end hangs down and coils toward your body. Blow into the tube, then suck the air out. Have someone take photos of you with the blower coiled and uncoiled. Prepare posters comparing photos of the coiled and uncoiled party blower with drawings of a butterfly's proboscis.

2. Different insects have different types of mouthparts. Observe the plierlike mouth of a cricket. Catch a cricket and place it in a plastic resealable vegetable bag with a small piece of bread and a small piece of sponge moistened with water. (See Chapter 4, "Jointed," for information on how to catch a cricket.) Use a magnifying lens to observe how the cricket eats the food. Within 60 minutes, release the cricket where you found it.

Find out more about the different mouthparts of insects. Prepare a display using materials to represent each mouthpart type, such as pliers for a cricket, a coiled party blower for a butterfly, and a sponge for a fly.

CHECK IT OUT!

Insects take food into their body through their mouthparts. Through digestion, the food is chemically changed to supply the body with *nutrients* (substances used by the body for growth, repair, and energy) and get rid of any waste products. Find out more about how insects digest food. What is a crop? A gizzard?

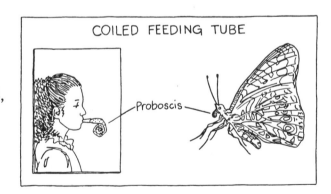

COILED FEEDING TUBE

Proboscis

13

Survivors

PROBLEM

How does color protect insects?

Materials

yardstick (meterstick)
4 pencils
at least 82 feet (24.6 m) of string
scissors
eight 12-inch (30-cm) chenille craft
  stems: 1 each of red, green, brown,
  black, white, orange, yellow, plus
  any other color you choose (These
  are commonly called pipe cleaners.)
timer
helper

Procedure

1. Find a large outdoor area with short
   grass. Measure a square with 20-foot

(6-m) sides. Place a pencil at each
corner of the square.

2. Tie one end of the string to one of the
   pencils. Loop the string around each
   of the 3 remaining pencils, and tie the
   free end to the first pencil to form a
   marked-off plot of grass.

3. Cut twenty-four ½-inch (1.25-cm)
   pieces of each color of pipe cleaner.

4. Without letting your helper see,
   spread the pieces as evenly as possible in the marked-off plot of grass.

5. Using the timer, instruct your helper
   to pick up as many of the pieces as
   possible in 1 minute.

6. Count and record the number of each
   color found.

7. Knowing that there should be 24
   pieces of each color, calculate the
   number of each color not found.

Results

Your helper found some colors more easily than others and probably did not find all of the pieces.

Why?

It is hard for your helper to find colors that blend in with the grass or soil. If the grass is the same shade of green as the colored pieces, your helper will have trouble distinguishing between the two. Some of the darker-colored pieces may blend in with the shadows of the grass or soil.

Insects with colors that blend in with their background are said to be camouflaged. **Camouflage** is color and/or patterns that conceal an object by matching its surroundings. Camouflage protects insects from their **predators** (animals that kill and eat other animals). For example, a bird that feeds on grasshoppers will have trouble spotting a green grasshopper on green grass.

In this activity, your helper represents a predator, and the colored pieces found represent the different insects the predator would eat. Coloring that helps to camouflage insects from predators is called **protective coloration**.

LET'S EXPLORE

1. How does the number of predators affect the survival rate of insects? Scatter the found pieces in the plot. Repeat the activity twice, first using 5 helpers, then 10.

2. How does the color of the background affect which insects survive? Repeat the original experiment, using a plot of ground, half of which is not grass. **Science Fair Hint:** Take photos of the procedure and display the results.

SHOW TIME!

Simulate the effect of protective coloration by preparing colored pieces of bread to represent differently colored insects. Peel off and discard the crust of 4 slices of white bread. Break each bread slice into 80 small pieces. Leave the pieces of 1 slice white, but color the others red, yellow, and green. For each color, mix together ¼ cup (63 ml) of tap water and 10 drops of food coloring in a bowl. Soak the pieces of bread in the colored water, then spread them out on separate trays. Allow them to air dry.

Choose an area with short grass where birds are often seen. Place 20 bread pieces from each of the 4 different colors on the grass. Spread each group in

a circle of about 12 inches (30 cm) in diameter. Space the circles about 6 feet (1.8 m) apart.

Leave the area for 4 hours, then return and count the number of pieces of each color that have not been eaten. Subtract this number from 20 to determine the number of pieces eaten for each color. Repeat this procedure three times on 3 different days. Calculate the average number of pieces of each color eaten during the four trials by adding the totals for each color and dividing that total by 4.

CHECK IT OUT!

Some moths have markings on their wings that look like huge eyes. These markings can frighten away predators and are a form of protective coloration called *warning coloration*. Find out more about different types of protective coloration and examples of each. What is mimicry?

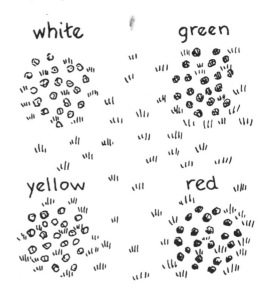

14

Singers

PROBLEM

How do some types of insects make sounds?

Materials

index card
fingernail file or emery board

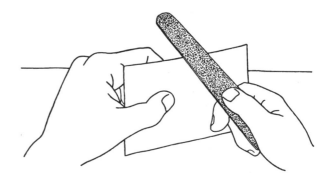

Procedure

1. Hold the index card upright with one long edge resting on a table.

2. Support the card with one hand as you draw the rough side of the file across the top edge of the card quickly two times.

3. Wait one second and repeat steps 1 and 2. (You can measure 1 second of time by saying "one thousand one.")

Results

You hear a rasping sound.

Why?

Sounds are caused when materials **vibrate** (move back and forth). When you rub the file across the paper, the rough surface of the file plucks the paper's edge, causing it to vibrate. The vibrating paper produces sound.

Certain insects, like crickets and grasshoppers, produce sounds in much the same way. These insects make sounds by rubbing two body parts, usually one sharp-edged and the other rough or filelike, against each other. This process is called **stridulation**. The short-horned grasshopper or locust stridulates by rubbing its rough hind leg across the sharp edge of its wing. Most insect sounds are made by males to attract females and to warn other males away.

LET'S EXPLORE

Most insect sounds do not get higher or lower, but remain constant throughout the sound. The sounds of related insect species are different because they have different **rhythms** (sounds in regular patterns). The length of time a sound is made and the time between sounds produces a rhythm. The rhythm in the experiment is the time between the sound produced by two quick strokes of the file across the card, silence for 1 second, then the sound of the two strokes again. Repeat the experiment, producing different rhythms. One way would be to first draw the file across the card very slowly two times. Then draw the file across the card quickly four to five times, followed by another second of silence before starting over.

SHOW TIME!

1a. Some insects produce sounds by **expelling** (forcing out) air or liquid from some body opening. Insects usually produce these sounds in response to disturbances. Some cockroaches produce a hissing sound by expelling air from certain **spiracles** (breathing holes) in their bodies. Demonstrate this type of sound production by holding your teeth together and blowing air between them.

b. The death's-head sphinx moth produces a whistling sound as it expels air from its **pharynx** (throat). Use a balloon to show how expelling air

can cause a whistling sound. Blow up the balloon and hold the open end with the index finger and thumb of both hands. Stretch the neck of the balloon outward to form a narrow opening and let the air out slowly.

2. Male cicadas produce very loud sounds by vibrating special **membranes** (thin, flexible sheets of tissue) called **tymbals**. The abdomen of the male cicada is almost completely hollow. The vibrating tymbals and the hollow abdomen act like a drum.

Demonstrate this method of sound production by cutting off the narrow part of a 12-inch (30-cm) round balloon. Stretch the bottom, rounded part of the balloon over

the mouth of a 10-ounce (300-ml) plastic glass. Pinch the center of the stretched balloon between the thumb and index finger of one hand. Pull the pinched balloon outward, then release it.

3. Insects also produce sound by vibrating their wings or other body parts. Bees and mosquitoes buzz because their wings vibrate. Use a vibrating index card to demonstrate the sound of an insect's vibrating wings. Stretch a rubber band around a 4-by-6-inch (10-by-15-cm) piece of cardboard. Place 2 pencils under the rubber band at opposite

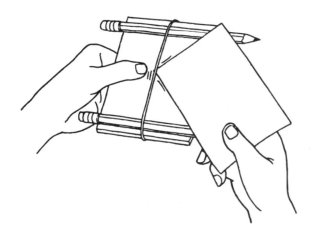

ends of the cardboard. Pluck the rubber band with your finger, then immediately touch the vibrating rubber band with the tip of an index card, which will make the index card vibrate. Use this and the other sound models to prepare a display for the different sound-producing mechanisms.

4. Create a display of each of the four methods of sound production described in this chapter: stridulating, expelling air, vibrating tymbals, and vibrating wings or other body parts. For each method, draw the model you made in each of the previous experiments along with a picture of an insect that uses that method to produce sound.

CHECK IT OUT!

Organs for hearing, or "ears," are never found on an insect's head. Many insects hear by means of fine hairs on different parts of their body. Find out more about how insects hear. Can only adult insects hear sounds? Where are the hairs or hearing organs located on insects' bodies?

15

Follow Me

PROBLEM

How do ants find food?

Materials

12-by-22-inch (30-by-55-cm) piece of
   white poster board
anthill with a few ants on the ground
   around it
4–6 rocks or other heavy objects
cracker
binoculars

Procedure

*CAUTION: Do not use fire ants for this
activity. Also, be sure not to stand on or too
near an anthill as you perform the activity.
Take special care not to allow ants to get
on your skin. If you are allergic to ant
strings, do not perform this activity.*

1. Lay the poster board on the ground
   with one end close to the entrance of
   the anthill.

2. Secure the paper with the rocks.

3. Crumble the cracker on the end of the
   paper opposite the entrance of the anthill.

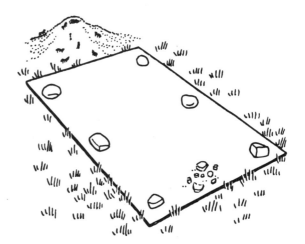

4. From a distance, use the binoculars to watch the ants and cracker crumbs for five minutes or more.

5. Return after 1 hour and again observe the ants and cracker crumbs.

Results

At first, a few ants examine the cracker crumbs. Some may carry a crumb back to the anthill, but others return without crumbs. After a time, many ants go back and forth, carrying crumbs to the anthill.

Why?

You may have noticed that the ants touch their antennae to the ground as they walk. This is because the ants smell through their antennae. The job of some ants is to go out and find food. They use their antennae to find the food, then return to the anthill, some with and some without food. As they return to the ant-hill, their bodies give off a chemical that leaves a scent on the ground.

The first ants "tell" the rest of the ants about the food. Scientists believe that ants communicate by touching their antennae together. The other ants use their antennae to follow the smell given off by the first ants back to the cracker crumbs.

The scented chemicals that ants and some other animals, especially insects, produce are called **pheromones**. These chemicals are produced inside the insect's body and **secreted** (given off) to the outside of the body. Pheromones are chemical signals used in communication among members of the same species.

LET'S EXPLORE

1. Determine if the ants that find food give the other ants information about the amount of food and the number of ants needed to carry it. Repeat the experiment, placing three piles of crumbs, each twice the size of the next, at three different places.

2. How would the ants respond if the scent trail were disrupted? Repeat the experiment by placing a 2-inch (5-cm)-wide strip of masking tape across the center of the poster board on the ground. After the ants have estab-lished a trail between the food and the anthill, remove the tape from the paper. Observe the behavior of the ants as they approach the disrupted area of the paper. **Science Fair Hint:** Take photos of the area around the anthill before and during the experiments and display them to represent the results.

SHOW TIME!

1. The firefly is actually a beetle with a light-producing chemical inside its abdomen called **luciferin**. Fireflies use light flashes to communicate with each other. Each species of firefly has

a different amount of time between flashes. Some female fireflies imitate the flashes of other species to lure the male fireflies close and then eat them.

Experiment with imitating the flashes of fireflies with a penlight. On a night when you see fireflies out, determine how many seconds occur between their flashes. (The easiest way to measure 1 second is to say "one thousand one.") Turn the penlight on and off at the determined time. Flash the light at least ten times.

2. The Austrian **entomologist** (scientist who studies insects) Karl von Frisch (1886–1982) contributed greatly to our understanding of how bees communicate with each other. He discovered that the female bees who leave the hive and find food do different types of dances. The dances inform other female members of the hive of the direction and distance of the food.

Find out more about bee dances. Prepare and display diagrams showing the different dances and how they indicate different directions and distances of food sources. For example, the two different dances in the diagram indicate different distances. The circular dance means food is close to the hive, and the wag-tail dance means food is far from the hive. As the bee moves through the figure-eight pattern in the wag-tail dance, she waggles her head and tail from side to side. The farther away the food is, the faster she waggles. Find out more about bee dancing. Are the dances the same for each species?

CIRCULAR DANCE

WAG-TAIL DANCE

short distance

long distance

CHECK IT OUT!

Female mosquitoes beat their wings to attract males. Find out more about courtship communication between insects.

16

Workers

PROBLEM

What kinds of ants live in an ant nest?

Materials

dressmaker's pin
1-gallon (4-liter) resealable plastic bag
close-fitting gardening gloves
long-handled mixing spoon
anthill
sheet of typing paper
desk lamp (optional)
magnifying lens
adult helper

Procedure

CAUTION: Do not use fire ants for this activity. Also, be sure not to stand on or too near an anthill as you perform the activity. Take special care not to allow ants to get on your skin. If you are allergic to ant stings, do not perform this activity.

1. Ask an adult to use the pin to make 20 to 30 small airholes through both layers around the top one-fourth of the bag.

2. Put on the gardening gloves and use the spoon to stir the top of the anthill.

3. When the ants run out of the ground, quickly scoop 2 to 3 spoonfuls of soil containing ants into the plastic bag. Immediately seal the bag and keep it sealed during the experiment.

4. Brush any ants off the outside of the bag and spoon with your gloved hand.

5. Lay the paper on a table near a window or under a desk lamp. Place the bag on the paper.

6. Without opening the bag, spread the soil in the bag to form a thin layer that covers the lower three-fourths of the

bag. The top one-fourth of the bag should have no soil.

7. Move the bag around to encourage some of the ants to walk across the area of no soil. Carefully press the bag down to hold an ant still while you study it with the magnifying lens. Study as many different ants as possible. Return the ants where you found them at the end of the experiment.

Results

The results will vary, but you probably found different kids of ants within the same nest.

Why?

Ants live in **colonies**, which are large groups of organisms of the same species living together and depending on each other. Each ant colony contains hundreds or even thousands of ants. The place

where the ants live is called a **nest**, and most ant nests are made of tunnels underground. Some ants build a hill of soil at the entrance to their underground nest, called an **anthill**.

Three different kinds of ants live in each ant colony: **queen, male,** and **worker.**

You most likely collected only worker ants. Sometimes workers in the same nest are different sizes. The smallest workers are generally smaller than the queen and males. The largest workers are called **soldiers**, and have unusually large, strong jaws. The soldiers help guard and defend the colony against enemies.

LET'S EXPLORE

1. How do worker ants of different species compare in size and shape? Repeat the experiment, collecting different species of ants. To find a variety of ant species, observe the ants outside different anthills in different locations where you live and in areas you visit. Remember to return the ants where you found them after observations are completed.

2. Use insect books to find information about the different ants that live in colonies, such as *The Fascinating World of Ants* by Angels Julivert (Hauppauge, NY: Barron's, 1991, pages 6–8). Use this information to identify the ants in your samples.
Science Fair Hint: Prepare two diagrams. Make one diagram comparing the queen, males, and worker ants. In the second diagram, compare different kinds of worker ants. Add information about each ant.

TYPES OF ANTS

Queen
· Spends her life laying eggs.
· Most ant colonies have more than one queen.
· Is not the ruler of the colony.
· Lives 10 to 15 years.

Male
· Does no work in the nest.
· Only duty is to mate with the queens.
· Hatches from unfertilized eggs.
· Lives a few weeks and dies soon after mating.

Workers
· Female ants.
· Do not mate or lay eggs.
· Some gather food, others clean, repair, and guard nest, while some take care of the queens and their young.
· Live 5 to 7 years.

SHOW TIME!

Prepare and observe your own ant colony. Place a small jar with a closed lid inside a larger jar. (The small jar will force the ants to stay near the sides of the larger jar, where you can see them.) Repeat the original experiment, but spoon the soil and ants into the larger jar. Fill the jar so that the soil is at least 2 inches (5 cm) below the mouth of the jar. Brush any ants off the outside of the jar with your gloved hand and cover the mouth of the jar with a knee-high stocking.

Set the jar in a large pan of water. (The water will help keep any ants that might eat through the stocking from leaving the jar.) Give the ants 1 day to get settled. Replace the stocking if it has holes. Place a small piece of moistened sponge on top of the soil. Scatter cracker or bread crumbs on the soil.

Put the ant colony in a place where it will not be disturbed. Be sure to keep it at room temperature and out of direct light. With a spoon, remove the old food and replace it with fresh food every other day. Keep the sponge moist with fresh water by removing it with a spoon and wetting it or by dropping water on it from an eyedropper. Observe the ants for a week or more, then return them to where you found them.

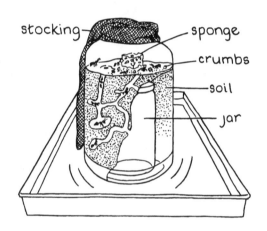

CHECK IT OUT!

Not all ants build nests in the ground. Spinner ants make their nests by connecting tree leaves together with silk woven by their larvae. The worker ants hold the larvae and move them back and forth across the connected leaves. Silk from larvae bonds the leaves together. Find out more about nest building by ants. Where do carpenter ants make their nests?

17

Builders

PROBLEM

How do termite mounds keep the insects inside cool?

Materials

scissors
30-gallon (113-liter) black plastic trash
    bag
toilet-tissue tube
ruler
masking tape
string
6 sharpened pencils
2 bulb-type thermometers
pen
paper

Procedure

1. Cut a hole in the bottom of the bag large enough to insert the toilet-tissue tube.

2. Insert all but about 1 inch (2.5 cm) of the tube into the hole in the bag. Gather the bottom of the bag around the tube and secure the bag to the tube with tape.

3. Place the bag in a sunny outdoor area. Tie the bag, tube side up, to a tree or other outdoor structure so that the bottom of the bag touches the ground.

4. Spread the mouth of the bag open. Use the 6 pencils as stakes to secure the bag to the ground, forming a plastic tentlike structure.

5. Read and record the temperature on each of the 2 thermometers.

6. Place one thermometer on the ground inside the plastic tent.

7. Tape the second thermometer, bulbside down, to the inside of the tube.

8. Read and record the two temperatures after 1 hour and every hour for 3 hours or more during the day.

Results

The temperature reading on the thermometer in the tube is higher than the temperature reading on the thermometer on the ground.

Why?

In your model, the temperature at the top of the plastic tent was greater than the temperature measured on the ground. This difference in temperature occurs because hot air rises. The hot air inside the plastic tent rises and passes over the thermometer in the tube as it exits the tent. Cooler air is then able to enter at the bottom of the tent.

Your plastic tent is a model of a termite mound, or nest. Termites are insects that can digest wood. Some termites build amazing nests. Your model represents the nest of African termites. These nests are towering aboveground mounds made of soil mixed with the termites' saliva. The mounds are designed to keep the insects inside cool. They have a central chimney, similar to the tube in your model. Openings in the lower part of the mound allow cooler air to enter. The cooler air circulates through the underground chambers beneath the mound. The warmer air exits through the chimney, keeping the mound cool.

LET'S EXPLORE

Would less air exiting the mound affect the temperature inside? Repeat the experiment, but cut the tube from top to bottom, overlap the edges, and tape them so the tube's opening is about one-half that of the original tube. **Science Fair Hint:** Find out how termites control the amount of air exiting their mound. Display diagrams showing the airflow.

SHOW TIME!

In tropical rain forests, termites such as African cubitermites build mushroom-shaped mud mounds. Determine how the shape of the mud mound is affected by the frequent rain in these forests. Use stiff paper, such as poster board, to prepare 2 differently shaped cones. Make a very steep cone and a gently sloped, umbrella-shaped cone.

Make mud to cover the cones. Termites make mud by mixing saliva with soil, but you can prepare yours by mixing garden soil and water. Cover each cone with a thick layer of mud. Allow each mound to dry thoroughly.

When dry, place the mounds on the ground. Place the umbrella-shaped mound on a coffee can or other large can to give it a mushroom shape. Use a watering can to represent rain. Hold the can about 8 inches (20 cm) from the top of each mound and pour the same amount of water across each. Take photos before, during, and after pouring the water. Use the photos as part of a project display to represent the results.

CHECK IT OUT!

The mounds of termites in northern Australia have four flat sides. Two of the sides are wide and two are narrow. Find out more about the mounds of these Australian compass termites. Why are they called compass termites? Do all termites build mounds above ground? For information about the nest building of termites, see Dr. Jennifer Owen's *Mysteries and Marvels of Insect Life* (London: Saffron Hill/Usborne, 1989), pages 18–19.

18

Hosts

PROBLEM

What's inside a gall?

Materials

tree with galls (Look for swellings on
the leaves and/or stems of a birch,
blueberry, huckleberry, elm, oak,
pecan, or willow tree.)
knife (to be used only by an adult)
cutting board
magnifying lens
adult helper

Procedure

1. With adult permission, remove 2 to 3
leaves or stems with galls from the
tree.

2. Ask your adult helper to cut 2 or 3 of
the galls in half.

3. Use the magnifying lens to observe
the contents of each gall.

Results

The gall may be empty or may contain
insects in various stages of development,
such as eggs, larvae, pupae, or adults.

Why?

A **gall** is an abnormal swelling or
thickening on a plant. Galls can occur
anywhere on a plant and may be nearly
solid or almost hollow.

Many galls are caused by gall-forming
insects. A gall forms when a female
insect lays her eggs in plant tissue. The
tissue of the plant grows rapidly around
the eggs, forming a bulge. This rapid tissue growth is the plant's reaction to
some **stimulus** (something that causes

activity or growth) from the insect. The insect that laid the eggs may have released a stimulus, such as growth-promoting fluids in saliva. A stimulus may also have been given off by the insects developing from the eggs.

After a brief period, the plant tissue stops growing. The eggs inside the gall develop into larvae and later into adults. The adult insects chew their way out of the gall, leaving tiny exit holes in the gall.

LET'S EXPLORE

1. Galls come in different sizes, shapes, and colors, depending on the insect and the plant. Repeat the experiment, using galls from different plants. **Science Fair Hint:** Make a poster showing a photograph of each host plant and a photograph of the gall on the plant. Use the poster as part of a project display.

2a. Observe the adult stage of gall-forming insects by watching galls and studying the adult insects that emerge. Many gall wasps form galls on oak trees. (Gall wasps are very small and, unlike some wasps, do not sting.) One type of gall wasp forms galls on oak trees in the summer, from which young wasps emerge in the fall or early winter. Another type of gall wasp forms galls in the spring, from which the wasps emerge in early summer.

Collect a few oak galls by breaking off the plant parts containing the galls and storing them in a large jar. Examine each gall before storing it to make sure the gall wasps have not already escaped through an exit hole. Cover the jar with a knee-high stocking. To keep the galls the same temperature as that of the outdoors, place the jar outdoors in a protected area, such as on a porch.

b. Would a different temperature affect the time it takes for the gall-forming insects in the previous experiment to develop? Repeat the previous experiment, placing the

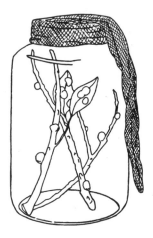

jar of galls in a different temperature from that of its normal environment.

SHOW TIME!

1. Symbiosis is a relationship between organisms of different species that have direct contact with each other. Find out more about gall-forming insects and their symbiotic relationships with plants. Are the relationships harmful to the plants? What are the different types of gall-forming insects? Prepare a display chart similar to the one shown.

COMMON GALL-FORMING INSECTS

Host Plant	Type of Gall	Symbiont (Gall-Forming Insect)
cypress	swellings on growing tips	gall midge fly
oak	leaf galls with orangish "hair"	hedgehog gall wasp
willow	conelike gall	willow cone gall fly

2. Look for galls on plants where you live and in areas you visit. Take pictures of each type of gall. Make note of the type of plant, where the plant is located (such as the city and/or state), and where the gall is located on the plant. This information will help you identify the photos later.

Study the photos and find out what insect made each type of gall. Use this information to prepare a single display for all photos or make a display for each photo. Make a stand-up display by bending a 10-inch (25-cm) -square piece of poster board in half. Attach the photo and information about the type of plant, location of plant, and type of insect as shown.

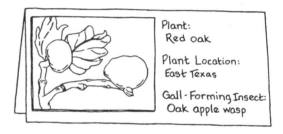

Plant:
Red oak

Plant Location:
East Texas

Gall-Forming Insect:
Oak apple wasp

CHECK IT OUT!

Parasites are organisms that live on or in host organisms. This symbiotic relationship is beneficial for the parasite, but harmful to the host. The larvae of ox warble flies live under the skin of their host. What effect does this have on the host? Find out about different parasitic insects, their effect on their hosts, and how they can be controlled.

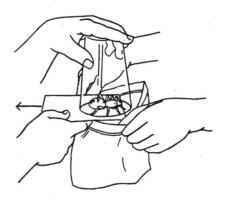

Relatives

PROBLEM

Are spiders insects?

Materials

pencil
1-gallon (4-liter) resealable plastic bag
garden spider in its web (Catch the
   spider by following the instructions
   below.).
10-ounce (300-ml) plastic cup
4-by-6-inch (10-by-15-cm) index card
spider field guide
magnifying lens
helper

Procedure

*NOTE: Keep the spider for the next experi-
ment, then return the spider to the ground
in the area where you found it.*

1. Use the pencil to make 10 to 15 small
   air holes around about one-fourth of
   the upper part of the bag.

2. Catch the garden spider (Araneidae)
   by covering it with the cup and at the
   same time moving the index card
   behind the web and over the mouth
   of the cup. *CAUTION: Use the spider
   field guide to make sure the spider is a
   garden spider.*

3. Ask your helper to hold the bag open. Hold the cup and card over the bag.

4. Slowly slide the card away so that the spider drops into the bag. Have your helper quickly seal the bag.

5. In a well-lighted area, use the magnifying lens to study and count the body parts and legs of the spider.

Results

The spider has two main body parts and eight legs.

Why?

You can tell from the number of body parts and legs that spiders are not insects. Insects have three main body parts and six legs, while spiders have two main body parts and eight legs. Spiders and insects are relatives. They are both arthropods, but spiders belong to a different group or class of arthropods called arachnids.

A spider's two main body parts are the **cephalothorax** (combined head and thorax) and the abdomen. Its four pairs of legs are attached to the cephalothorax. Like insects, spiders have an exoskeleton. Unlike insects, spiders do not have wings or antennae.

Spiders and insect larvae have a silk-spinning **organ** (a body part with a specific function) called a **spinneret**. There are usually six of these short, fingerlike organs located near the end of the underside of the spider's abdomen. Most spiders have eight eyes, but some have fewer. The eyes are located on the top and front of the head. The size, number, and position of the eyes vary among different species.

The garden spider is in a family of spiders called **orb weavers**. These spiders spin **orb webs**, which are webs in a design that looks like a wheel. Spokes of silk thread extend from the center and are connected by spirals of silk thread.

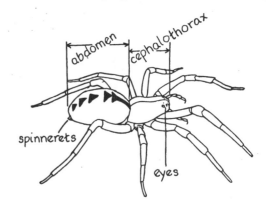

LET'S EXPLORE

Spiders generally release a silk thread, called a drag line, everywhere they go. Lay the bag and spider on a sheet of dark construction paper. Look for silk threads in the bag. Turn the bag over so that the spider is on its back. Look for the spinnerets, which are finger-like structures near the end of the abdomen. *Very gently* push the bag against the spinnerets and watch them move.

SHOW TIME!

1. Make a clay spider model. Use spider field guides, reference books, and encyclopedias for information about the spider's different body parts. Make the clay by combining 2 cups (500 ml) of flour, ¾ cup (188 ml) of water, and ½ cup (125 ml) of salt. Knead the clay for about 2 minutes to make it soft and moldable. A spider does not have bones; its exoskeleton gives it support. But you can use toothpicks to give support to their legs in the model. For each of the eight legs, mold clay around a toothpick, then break the toothpick in four places, leaving the wood partially attached to form the joints in the leg. Smooth the clay over the joints. Let the clay air-dry several days to harden or ask an adult to bake the clay at 250°F (121°C) for 90 minutes or until it is hard.

   Make a legend to display with the model. Include on the legend information about each body part shown on the model, such as:

   - **cephalothorax:** Combined head and thorax. Contains the brain, poison glands, and stomach.

   - **abdomen:** Contains the heart, digestive tract, reproductive organs, respiratory organs, and silk glands.

2. Spiders hatch from eggs and usually look like tiny adults. Find out more about the development of spiders. Make a poster comparing spider development to the complete and gradual metamorphoses of insects.

CHECK IT OUT!

1. Spinnerets are found in both insects and spiders. Find out more about spinnerets. How does the organ differ in location and function in these two organisms?

2. Spiders mainly eat insects. But spiders do not have mouthparts that chew, so they can only eat liquids. Use reference books or encyclopedias to find out how spiders turn the solid body of an insect into a liquid meal.

20

Snares

PROBLEM

Are all the silk threads in an orb web the same?

Materials

scissors
black construction paper
small round plastic container, such as
   an empty, clean cottage cheese or
   margarine container
orb web (Use a spider field guide to
   identify an orb web. These webs are
   often found between tree branches
   or porch pillars.)
scissors
desk lamp
magnifying lens
adult helper

Procedure

CAUTION: Make sure the spider isn't in the web before doing the experiment.

1. Cut a circle from the construction paper to fit in the bottom of the plastic container and place it in the container.

2. Place the mouth of the container against the spiderweb.

3. Push the container forward to break off the part of the web covering the mouth of the container. Ask your helper to use the scissors to cut web strands so that the web is stretched across the mouth of the container.

4. Place the container under the lamp.

5. Use the magnifying lens to study the strands of the web stretched across the mouth of the container. *NOTE: Keep the web-covered container for the following experiments.*

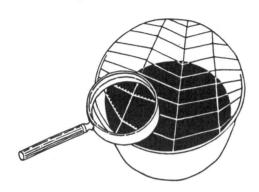

Results

Some of the threads are smooth and some look like a beaded necklace.

Why?

The silk threads in a spiderweb are different. Some spider silk dries when air touches it and some silk stays sticky. The sticky beaded thread you saw was made from a combination of dry and sticky silk. Silk flows out of tiny holes in the spider's spinnerets. The spinnerets move in fingerlike motions as they coat a dry silk thread with sticky silk. The spider then uses the claws on its legs to pluck the thread. The plucking causes the liquid silk to separate into tiny beads along the thread.

LET'S EXPLORE

1. Are only the beaded threads in a spider's web sticky? Use the eraser of a pencil to test the stickiness of the different threads of the web-covered container from the original experiment. Place the container under the desk lamp. Carefully touch a smooth web thread with the eraser, then lift the pencil. Repeat the procedure, touching a beaded thread. Sticky threads will stick to the eraser and be lifted.

2. Why don't spiders get stuck in their webs? Spiders won't stick if they walk only on the threads that are not sticky. Oil on their feet keeps them from sticking to sticky threads. Demonstrate how oil keeps a spider from sticking to its web. Repeat the previous experiment, wetting the pencil eraser with cooking oil.

3. Sticky silk does not dry, but it can become covered with dust and lose its stickiness. Squeeze a container of body powder so that the powder is sprayed over the silk threads. Use a dry pencil eraser to test the stickiness of the powder-covered threads.

SHOW TIME!

1. The orb web is the most common type of spiderweb. An orb web looks like a wheel with silk spokes that extend out from the center and are connected by spirals of silk thread. Make a model of an orb web. Find a small, dead tree branch about 2 feet (0.6 m) long with at least two branches. Follow the directions on a plaster of paris package to fill a small coffee can about three-fourths full with plaster. Mix the plaster in the can. Place the bottom of the branch in the wet plaster and keep the branch upright until the plaster dries.

Form the frame of the web. Tie a crochet thread to the upper part of one branch (point A) and stretch the thread across to the second branch (point B) to form the bridge line. Wrap this thread around different parts of the branches to end up back at point A as shown. Don't break the thread.

Create a Y shape inside the frame by draping the thread loosely between points A and B. Cut and tie the thread at point B. Attach a short piece of thread to the center of the draped thread and attach it to the frame thread below to complete the Y shape as shown.

Tie several threads to the center of the Y, then attach them to the frame. These threads extending out from the center are the **radial lines** of the web. Attach a long, spiraling thread around the radial lines. Devise a method of attaching the spiraling thread. One method is to lay the model on several sheets of newspaper. Add drops of glue to the radial lines, then lay the thread in a spiral pattern on the glue. Allow the glue to dry before standing the web up. Display your orb web model.

2. You were able to tie and stretch the thread between the branches to make the orb web model. Find out how orb weavers attach and stretch silk thread between the branches. Make and display a poster showing diagrams of the different steps it takes a spider to weave an orb web. Include pictures of orb weavers.

CHECK IT OUT!

Spiderwebs come in different designs. Cobwebs are shapeless, tangled webs often found around houses. Find out more about web designs and the spiders that weave them. Which spiders spin the following kinds of webs: platform, bowl-and-doily, triangle, filmy dome, and labyrinth?

Appendix

Catalog Suppliers of Insects

Carolina Biological Supply Company
(CB)
2700 York Road
Burlington, NC 27215
1-800-334-5551

Delta Education (DE)
P.O. Box 3000
Nashua, NH 03061-3000
1-800-442-5444

Frey Scientific/Division of Beckley
Cardy
100 Paragon Parkway
Mansfield, OH 44903
1-800-225-3739

Insect Field Guides

Borror, Donald J., and Richard E. White. *A Field Guide to Insects: America North of Mexico.* Peterson Field Guide series. Boston: Houghton Mifflin, 1970.

Farrand, John, Jr. *National Audubon Society Pocket Guide: Insects and Spiders.* New York: Knopf, 1995.

Forey, Pamela, and Cecilia Fitzsimons. *An Instant Guide to Insects.* New York: Crescent Books, 1987.

Leahy, Christopher. *Peterson First Guide to Insects of North America.* Boston: Houghton Mifflin, 1987.

Levi, Herbert W. *Spiders and Their Kin.* New York: Golden Press, 1990.

McGavin, Dr. George C. *Insects of North America.* San Diego: Thunder Bay Press, 1995.

McKeever, Susan. *Butterflies of North America.* San Diego: Thunder Bay Press, 1995.

Pyle, Robert Michael. *National Audubon Society Field Guide to North American Butterflies.* New York: Knopf, 1981.

Zim, Herbert S., and Clarence Cottam. *Insects.* New York: Golden Press, 1987.

Books

Chinery, Michael. *Life Story: Ant.* Mahwah, NJ: Troll, 1991.

Dashefsky, H. Steven. *Entomology.* New York: TAB Books, 1994.

Julivert, Angels. *The Fascinating World of Ants.* Hauppauge, NY: Barron's, 1991.

Kneidel, Sally. *Pet Bugs.* New York: Wiley, 1994.

Mound, Lawrence. *Insects.* Eyewitness Books series. New York: Dorling Kindersley, 1990.

Potter, Jean. *Nature in a Nutshell for Kids.* New York: Wiley, 1995.

Pringle, Laurence. *The Golden Book of Insects and Spiders.* New York: Western, 1990.

Russo, Monica. *The Insect Almanac.* New York: Sterling, 1992.

Scott, James A. *The Butterflies of North America.* Stanford, CA: Stanford University Press, 1986.

Suzuki, David. *Looking at Insects.* New York: Wiley, 1991.

Wellnitz, William R. *Science in Your Backyard.* Blue Ridge Summit, PA: TAB Books, 1992.

Glossary

abdomen   The rear part of an insect or spider's body.

amylase   A chemical found in saliva that breaks down starch into less complex chemicals.

Animal Kingdom   The largest classification group for all animals and the one in which arthropods belong.

antenna (plural **antennae**)   Long, thin, movable sensory part on the head of an insect and certain other arthropods used to feel, smell, and sometimes, to hear.

anthill   A hill of soil at the entrance to an underground ant nest.

arachnids   Arthropod group containing spiders.

Arthropoda   The phylum for five classes of organisms: insects, arachnids, crustaceans, millipedes, and centipedes.

arthropod   Any animal in the Arthropoda phylum. Animals without backbones that have jointed legs and segmented bodies covered by an exoskeleton.

Bernoulli's principle   The natural law that states that when any fluid, such as air, flows across a surface, its pressure on the surface decreases as its speed increases.

camouflage   Colors and/or patterns that conceal an object by matching its background.

caterpillar   The larva of a butterfly or moth.

centipede   An arthropod group consisting of organisms that are wormlike and have one pair of legs per body segment.

cephalothorax   The combined head and thorax of a spider.

cerci (singular **cercus**)   A pair of structures at the rear of an insect's abdomen. May be clasperlike, feelerlike, or absent.

chitin   A lightweight, relatively hard, but generally flexible material in the exoskeleton of arthropods.

class   A subdivision of a phylum. Contains one or more orders.

classification   The arrangement of things into groups according to ways in which they are alike.

cobweb   A shapeless, tangled spiderweb.

colony   A group of organisms, such as ants, that live together and interact.

complete metamorphosis   See **metamorphosis, complete**.

compound eye   The large eye of an insect, containing thousands of ommatidia.

contraction   Squeezing together.

coxa   The leg segment connected to an insect's body.

crustacean   An arthropod group including water dwellers, such as crabs, shrimps, and lobsters, and land dwellers, such as wood lice.

darkling beetle   An often dark-colored beetle that eats vegetable matter. The larval stage is known as a *mealworm*.

digest   To break down food into an absorbable form.

dormant   In a state of being inactive.

egg   First phase of metamorphosis.

entomologist   A scientist who studies insects.

exoskeleton   The outer covering of arthropods. External skeleton made mostly of chitin.

expelling   Forcing out.

facets   Lenses at the surface of the ommatidia of an insect's compound eye.

family   A subdivision of an order. Contains one or more genera.

femur   The second main section of an insect's leg.

gall   An abnormal swelling or thickening on a plant, often caused by a gall-forming insect.

genera (singular **genus**)   Subdivisions of families. Contain one or more species.

gradual metamorphosis   See **metamorphosis, gradual**.

habitat   The physical place, such as a forest, grassy field, pond, or desert, where a plant or animal lives.

head   The front part of an insect or spider's body.

incomplete metamorphosis   See **metamorphosis, gradual**.

indigenous   Native to a certain area.

insect   An organism with three main body parts, three pairs of legs, and usually one or two pairs of wings. Belongs to the Animal Kingdom, the phylum Arthropoda, and the class Insecta.

Insecta   The class to which insects belong.

instars   The stages between molts of larvae.

invertebrates   Animals without backbones.

jointed   Consisting of different parts that fit together.

kingdom   The largest group into which organisms are classified.

larva (plural **larvae**)   An immature insect in the second stage of complete metamorphosis which differs greatly from the adult.

larval stage   The second stage in complete metamorphosis. An active, feeding stage.

leaf litter   Layers of newly fallen and partially decayed leaves covering the soil beneath trees or bushes.

lens   The part of the eye that focuses light rays.

luciferin   A chemical that produces light.

male ants   Winged ants that are smaller than the queen ant. Their only function is to mate with the queen. They live only for a few weeks and die soon after mating.

mealworm   The larva of a darkling beetle.

membrane   Thin, flexible sheet of tissue.

membranous   Resembling a thin, flexible sheet of tissue paper.

metamorphosis, complete   The four-stage process of insect development from egg to larva to pupa to adult.

metamorphosis, gradual   The three-stage process of insect development from egg to nymph to adult. Also called **incomplete metamorphosis**.

millipede   An arthropod group consisting of organisms that are wormlike and have two pairs of legs per body segment.

molting   The process of shedding an exoskeleton.

mouthparts   The body parts near an insect or spider's mouth used for gathering and eating food.

nectar   A sugary liquid produced in many flowers at the base of their petals, which is food for many insects.

nest   A place where colonies of insects, such as ants and termites, live.

nymph   An insect in the second stage of incomplete metamorphosis. The nymph is smaller than the adult and wingless.

ocelli   The simple eyes of insects, which can see the difference between light and dark but cannot see images.

ommatidium (plural **ommatidia**)   A section of an insect's compound eye that includes the facet.

orb weaver   One of a family of spiders that spin orb webs.

orb web   The most common spiderweb, which has a design that looks like a wheel with spokes of silk thread extending from the center and connected by spirals of thread.

order   A subdivision of a class. Contains one or more families.

organ   A body part with a specific function.

organism   A living thing.

ovipositor   An egg-laying structure at the rear of a female insect.

pharynx   Throat.

pheromones   Scented chemicals secreted to the outside of the body which cause certain behavior by other individuals of the same species.

phylum (plural **phyla**)   A subdivision of a kingdom. Contains one or more classes.

predator   An animal that kills and eats other animals.

pressure   A force acting on a surface.

proboscis   The tubelike, sucking mouthpart of some insects, such as moths and flies.

protective coloration   Coloring that helps to protect insects from predators.

pupa (plural **pupae**)   An insect in the third stage of complete metamorphosis.

pupal stage   The nonfeeding and generally inactive third stage of complete metamorphosis.

pupate   To form a pupa.

queen ant   The mother ant of an ant colony. She is the largest ant in the colony and spends her long life, some 10 to 15 years, laying eggs.

radial lines   Lines extending from the center to the frame of an orb web.

rhythm   Sound in a regular pattern.

scales   Tiny, lightweight, flattened hairs on the wings of butterflies and moths.

secrete To give off.

simple eye *See* ocelli.

soldier ants The largest worker ants, with strong jaws used to defend the colony against enemies.

species A subdivision of a genus. A group of organisms that are the same kind and can produce offspring.

spider An organism in the arachnid class. A small animal with a body divided into two parts, four pairs of jointed legs, usually eight simple eyes, and no antennae.

spinneret A silk-spinning organ that is a short fingerlike structure located near the end of the underside of a spider's abdomen.

spiracles Breathing holes in the body of an insect.

starch A complex chemical found in foods.

stimulus Something that causes activity or growth.

stridulation The process by which insects make sounds by rubbing two body parts, such as one sharp-edged and the other rough or filelike, against each other.

symbiosis A relationship between organisms of different species that have direct contact with each other.

tarsus The fourth and outermost main section of an insect's leg.

thorax The middle part of an insect's body.

tibia The third main section of an insect's leg.

tymbal A hard, vibrating membrane in insects such as cicadas that produces sound.

veins A framework of thickened ridges in an insect's wings.

vibrate To move back and forth.

wing pad A small winglike growth on a nymph.

worker ants Female ants that vary in size and do not mate or lay eggs. They are responsible for all the nest chores, defend the nest, and live for 5 to 7 years. The largest workers that defend the nest are called soldiers.